CATHEDRAL
OF
WISH

CATHEDRAL
OF
WISH

Cammy Thomas

Four Way Books
New York City

Distributed by
University Press of New England
Hanover and London

Editorial Office
Four Way Books
POB 535, Village Station
New York, NY 10014
www.fourwaybooks.com

Library of Congress Catalogue Card Number: 2004101057

ISBN 1-884800-63-7

Cover art by Brian Rumbolo
By permission of the artist.

Cover design by Pablo A. Medina for Cubanica

This book is manufactured in the United States of America and
printed on acid-free paper.

 Publication of this book is made possible in part by
an award from the National Endowment for the Arts,
NATIONAL which believes that a great nation deserves great art,
ENDOWMENT
FOR THE ARTS and by a generous grant from a private foundation

Four Way Books is a not-for-profit organization. We are grateful
for the assistance we receive from individual donors, foundations,
and government arts agencies.

Distributed by University Press of New England
One Court Street, Lebanon, NH 03766

Acknowledgments

I am grateful to the following publications in which these poems first appeared, sometimes in somewhat different form:

88: A Journal of Contemporary American Poetry: "Autumnal"

The Aurorean: "Good-Bye She Said"

Blaze: "Romance is Fatal," "Vacation," "Planting"

Marlboro Review: "The Mysterious Stranger"

Mystic River Review: "Bone-Eater"

Pine Island Journal of New England Poetry:
    "First Trip Since the Disaster"

Sahara: "One Loss," "You Haven't"

South Boston Literary Gazette: "Snake"

For their wisdom and support, I wish to thank my extended family, along with Cynthia Anderson, Ramsay Breslin, Carl Dennis, Ann Keniston, Julia Lisella, Gail Mazur, Heather McHugh, Martha Rhodes, Theodora Stratis, Augusta Thomas, Dorothy Thomas, Ellen Bryant Voigt, Alan Williamson, Eleanor Wilner, Rosamond Zimmermann, and the greater community of the Warren Wilson College MFA Program. And I thank, in memoriam, Sara Doniach and Bart Wasserman.

for Tony, Emma, and Claire

Table of Contents

Hunting

his black days he fed us pheasant
shot in fields behind the house
mudroom shotgun oiled black
slick bolt pulled back

hung the birds
in the garage to season
trembled as he plucked
their blue-green plumes

oh it tasted tender
that darkest meat
squawk and talon
sometimes we spat a pellet or two

Fall

my father pushed our wrought iron
love-seat off the terrace into a circle

of bronze roses it fell out of a family picture
my father dismayed again amazed at himself

in the love-seat a boy
not yielding trying to keep

his bare feet on the flagstones
my brother flipped over shouting

"From My Father's Heart I Sprung"

—Eavan Boland

from my father's heart I sprung
never got my heart
searched the woods at night
apart

he taught me how to hear a chord
shout out loud
never doubt the lonely
word

when I learned to sing he said
don't follow me
search for a dazzled silent
sea

I ride in sculpted armor red
girl with sword
blank eyes winged helmet, pregnant
head

In My Mother's Bed

for A.M.T.

that is all ye know on earth she said
smoothing crinkled pages
of the book once dropped in the bath

    in a darkened room
she read to me
how the sun came up on the left
and the boards did shrink
        oh tiger she said

    I don't know where my father slept
I think she wanted

to be still and sick
as she tended me

sun-barred blankets
twined acanthus bedposts
damp white sheets

a stately pleasure dome she said
    mother I thought pleasure
her nipples dark under the nightgown
that sunny dome those caves of ice

at night he built a fire in our bedroom
grating roar
    blue walls a sea
books in the shelves breathing
titles sliding like snakes

I turned over for an alcohol rub
poured freezing over my back
she fanned it
      colder
    lifeless ocean

he said when will this be over
she said when

Bath

the razor slid up her leg
stroke and stroke
vanishing the invisible

steam rising, belly flat, breasts afloat
soap a bubbled slick
dunked her head and came up spraying

glassy beads on floor and wall
dark hair plastered seal-like
sank to rinse and stood sheeting

water fell, turbaned the towel
lay covered on her too large bed
wet spot on her pillow

sweat sliding at her throat
sheet keeping away
drifting currents of cold

The Quiet Boy

the quiet boy
with eyes like a landslide
sits under his hat
watching his baby sister get beaten

One Loss

there's only one loss
red spilling out of blue
trees and roads rolling by

my mother reassured me but what sealed
our separation was her love

clouds swim into shapes of human things
the sun's reflections follow a girl
swimming in silver reservoir
each kick a flake of light

in the woods as many animals live
as people in a city
light on lights off—stone beehive

red two-inch biplane prehistoric
dragonfly I separate from you
red spills out into blue

Harm or Home You Can Only Make One

why did he descend on her
eagle to little brown wren

beneath his vermilion dives
talons pulling prey from the lake

he wanted a sweetness not himself
when he covered her she gasped

if she flew all day
he found her in a moment

the seeds she found not enough
her own young ravished her warm breast

Axe and Adze

what most moved him
pushed us from ourselves
a children's chorus razed
each rest a bloody death

what he needed
fell on us like blows

rage with no referent
kitchen of meat and wine
tip of knife

beauty the thinner that bled
our tulip hearts ready to spill

love the best backdrop
for axe and adze

Again

I lean over my dinner plate,
dreams zigzagging 'til I ache
in black armor,
waiting for him to confess.

Green bottleflies sit on the sill
buzzing me to death.

He said his car exploded
passport burned
light out couldn't get home—
his words.

Credit

how measure my debt
if not from safe remove

take my old half self
and send to the moon

Mom Slid Into Her Glass

Mom slid into her glass
dim eyes through coppery Scotch
heavy old-fashioned
completely contained her

then I was metal
silver-hinged girders
impervious aerodynamics
a 'bot with a 'bot's shocked face

I picked up the glass
which slid to a gap
in my cold chest
and stuck

doubled over
twisted bent upended
I tried to budge her
but she stayed glassed

unmelting metal
I couldn't smash her
stuck fast she mewed like a cat
caught like a stream by a rock

God's Hand

she shivered almost open
among melons and music

gave herself to bravery
no pain just gasp

they took too long
to find the small vein

where did she hide so quiet

Moving Day

Who needs remains—

neat bricks for a brutal building
in some fierce new downtown?

Not as good as death, you stars
glimmering in glass,
you small remaining drops
of clear reprieve.
Why make me leave my known—?

He moved me to some heaven,
jettisoned my books my hands—

just sky as far as I can see.

The Old Childs House

empties smashed against the bricks
fountains of white roses splash
into dry swimming pool

weeping beech's tangled branches
shutters nailed shut
against screaming jays

blank-eyed heads on cornices
muddy feet streak dusty floors
rococo radiators whanged with sticks

black-eyed susans spool yellow
through windows of the sacred kitchen
rusted beater and scraper

Violin in the Underworld

I'm only a baby when I
first play for him
    my avid intimate listener

Prokofiev's Sonata in D for instance
how darkness wells out of light—the bitter
    taste of pomegranate

I put myself here
the only sweetness I have
    clamps me to him

Suicide Seeds

grow sterile plants
perfect buds of sex and death
were we made never to mingle
children coming from far away

unrealized blessings
produced too easily
random seed dropping into mysteries
of happy sad sick or well

suicide trees would they flower without seeds
flower at all
is that blankness
or the futureless heart of things

if it's only once
will we ever recognize
what can spring from nothing
we will have no ancestors

Every Morning a Parting

blue branches of trees bend
around the island swim nervous dogs

Dorothy waves her naked doll
the sides of the world warm in the sun

above birds ride waves of wind
train blows a hole through the tunnel

mother's a beacon in space
father's away at a lighted window

when dark birds of the air clang down
and yellow buses ride past fisted statues

the sides of the world
how they doze in the sun

she wanders past stinging nettles
bells chime through her sleep

In the Library

1. Kiss

every night he lifted his daughter
to kiss the ivory whale
above the library door

2. Rack of Guns

that time the boy heard
his mother being hit again
swung the cabinet open, one
fell into his hand oiled and heavy
sighted on his father's shocked face

what were you aiming at
grabbed the boy's thumbs and bent
them back until they snapped

3. "The Whiteness of the Whale"

broke from the horizoning sea

keelhauled cabinboy saw God's foot
on the treadle of the loom

stern old God the father
ashed his cigar
in a silver porringer

4. "Muskrat Ramble"

in and out of hotels
he'd done it with the horsey set
those ready red–haired girls
bevies of sisters

in the background Louis'
bluesy something
just keep moving
raise it to your lips

5. Goodnight

after she left again
he reclined mystified
among dark hunting scenes
Casals grinding on
everything of sorrow and glory
left him to his bitter Twain

Reconciliations

in weeks between bouts
big house shaking

their faces eager or dying
or indifferent

how many times has their bed
turned empty

something coiling and jeweled
twisting in the dark

sad men in boots lifting it
and lifting it again

Midnight Garden

evening primrose closes
no one passes
quiet except my clippers in the roses

shrouded house sleeps
sister bedded with her cats, blasted
stern father swooned

Cracked Sycamore

cracked sycamore
turn the moon blue
kill the lights
in this wish house

mother get more
heavy blankets
hot in the dark
clock stopped

father goes soused
outage mother
crouch over your candle
dreaming camellias

eyes shut ice picks

Snake

today mom comes outside
she's dry but doesn't look well
wants us to stop talking

we discuss the weedy pond
having nothing left to offer
except politeness

at the outdoor fireplace
marooned by stones
she scoops up something

nothing to it she says
as it writhes in the air
and we back away admiring

The Children

A marble forgotten
under the table.

The sweeter their smiles,
the deeper my sorrow.

Combing their hair,
I weep on them secretly.

When they leave,
I make myself wave.

Inheritance

the birds sing their repeated Greek as if they thought
why does rose bend its layered head this way
face in the window my mother's face
birds emptying out of the trees
moon dial of the grandfather clock stopped
at 12:27—our commemorative pictures
their glossy flesh-denying flatness
broken clock red chairs waving bathers
mallards at the edge of the cold pond
love as imposition as embarrassment
as if not knowing would be better for us children
her deafness makes music sound like screaming birds

It must be love but funny it's such a solitary thing,
all of them gone, barely speaking. My children
made treasures of the cheap red chairs.
Out the train window fields of dead stalks,
here heat blasting me—blessed warmth—
the pheasants know how to avoid hunters in these fallow fields.
If the clock were fixed, there'd be a lever
to turn off its chimes. I walk home in darkness,
trees leaning in, hard light the eye of a bird.

Romance Is Fatal

not just to oneself
the hectic flush not covered
but removed, a surgery
a change of view

dream horses and dolls
she snatches to show us
our willingness to bribe
ourselves away

the properties and ponies
our lives lie upon

she says all winter fevers must be iced

only to keep our havoc from ourselves
keep the world sweet and wondering
for children as nice as these

For This

you offer a small white dog
to lie at my feet
say you'll train him
never to leave me

a lady accompanied
by a small white dog

oh dog my broken heart
empty holder
lonely evangelist

Wrack

she tried to keep us
from the wreck of wanting

anyway it stayed a gun within
hot lead pressed against

unseen mortal wound
I steel myself

shelving fortune
flee to foursquare

At Dinner

I could've called her
to come and take us home
but I was proud and she was sad

he sat us to a nightly ritual of grief
loading the gun
laying it on the table

Family Day at the Rehab

they tell us not to talk not to think
just *be with yourselves*

my mother whispers to me
can you hear that river?

Hollow

he asked if I was going to the party
and I said what party

when my mother said I mustn't mind
the trees waved each alone

the dolls stood up declaring
don't tell us who we are

trying to be kind the doctor
leaned over smiling death

Bone-Eater

that lawyer of the living room who ate our bones for tea
and told us we should be glad, who gave us
our heart's desire then snatched it away, who played
games in the rain smacking us with the heavy ball
until we swallowed our laughter

his doctors are removing him piece by piece
while he composes oral arguments from his bed
explaining which pieces will go and how and why

he doesn't know why no one comes
to distract him from the stench
rising from his robe

look my sister says
as he limps away in his johnny
he has that same tiny ass we all have

His Gifted Children

left him

the sun speared its hot wings
across the mown field
where they hid from him

a god in his underwear
conducting the stick instruments
he'd fathered

Dismasted

The doctors tossed my stones, left me
an empty jacket, some revenge
for many days with those my mother
would have shunned and wife undone.
They were lovely though, the comfy
and the starved, the stately and the small.

I especially loved to make the nasty
ones moan, to sneak at night
under someone's roof, take his wife
after a g&t with slice of lime.
I'm not your modern home wrecker
sneaking around with someone ready to go—
my in-out was quick as a gasp
in the next room.

I'd enter them standing,
shy as horses, smooth backs arching,
here and here and here.

Autumnal

the instruments don't notice
the cold seeping under the door
at a turn in the road he sees
trees red overhead

the end of purity of the body
to live in layers
of cities built on ruins

then the straightaway home
stone wall pruned shocked pines
the field across the street
its stale pond filled with dogs

The Two

booze brokering
synapses into somewhere broken

or carved by cancer
shoulder bones showing

I heard the alarm ringing
pickled tubed mother
doctors are better than home
hospital saves me from seeing her

I watched him vomit
in a pail with a hole in the bottom
leave it outside in the snow
and die before summer

she's not dead just damaged
godbottle hollowing a hole

turn down the morphine he asked me
the day he died said he was writing
an essay in his head on Shakespeare
and the *Book of Common Prayer*
didn't want the yellow kitty cat to come

terrible things came out of them
from the kiln that fires love impermeable

Almost Gone

I knew we'd end up here
where I wash my hands *after* touching you

your green eyes blink at me
well up but do not spill

the pneumatic boots on your prone legs
fill and empty simulating walking

Good-Bye She Said

good-bye again
and nuzzled my neck
as mothers sniff their babies
nuzzled my face
to touch her child
while death waited

was it the alcohol
letting her show me
what she worked so hard to hide
her cheek slack
and tender against mine

One Always Beside Us

(for Elly)

our middle sister sees
our world until she
unfurls us waiting

still in the beating
the weeping she makes
an opening hoping

bad burden to think
to say for all five this
is too much that'll do

her eyes age even
before she knows how
to love what to save

what grave withholding
kept our father from
her small straight law

how help one who
saw them coming
wouldn't bow

Not Fade Away

in his rented garden he grows
acrid marigolds four feet high
with flowers big as faces
and squashes whose vines twine up the trees—
you'd have to climb for the fruit

his mother's old car coughs
in the garage on bald wheels

sitting on a sprung silk sofa
he puts back another beer
headset cranking the Dead
"Not Fade Away"
flowers so bright at dusk they sting his eyes

his roses bloom impossibly
hot red heads pushing perfume
past canes of thorns

Vacation

my sisters come for dinner
of lobsters cracked with a hammer

when it rains we swim in the pool
where a few toads die every night
mornings we get the skimmer
and flip them into the woods

under boiling white clouds
the orchestra plays
Overture to "The Wasps"

all night the fan goes
sounding like a highway

in the fields bees refuse
to return to their tiny cells

Planting

Appetite quite gone.
Last time I weighed this
I was twenty.
Can't walk
to the end of the driveway
to see the bulbs I planted last fall—

small white narcissus,
red tulips,
*   not the tulips*
that bloom in my gut.

Careless waving of trees,
*   bendy birch,*
the crows who come
to eat the seed I throw
don't know I'm dying.

And look:
the sun curves round the world
as if it matters.

"The Mysterious Stranger"
—Mark Twain

in this long exercise how one comes
at last to the naming of parts

on his back, toes slightly pointed
hair lacquered in place
one finger that can't straighten itself
hungry face made smooth
in death, gentle now like his son's face
dread and power flown

under a hospital blanket
head not feeling the pillow
hands stiff, cold from the freezer
he's finally silent

those stuck-shut eyes used to roam the world
insatiable—how often he got up
during dinner, church, anything
and rushed out smoking
something always chasing him

he burned his people
to ashes from time to time
had since he was a boy, when he'd gallop away
fear and pain transferred
to the quivering creature beneath him

we rose for him like fish to bait
hooked like chumps on thrills

hard to look on the silence to come
anguish dimmed but with it rapture, dazzle

Burial

emptying sky
water over icy roads
crusts of snow
rotted boat

widows, steps, halves, wholes
on the edge of his muddy pond

Through the long night watches

his disinherited sons
pour his ashes disappearing
salamander ooze

May thine angels spread

black embraces

Their white wings above me

house breathes the end
of a terrible love story

Watching round my bed

dark exhalations
get out get out

Snakeskin

after he died
I found his suits hung up
dried flowers still in buttonholes
suspenders attached and dangling

I Felt Fierce Love Envelop
after Robert Hayden

after wine and weeping
in my father's cathedral of wish
magic cemetery of meaning

his fiery words sharpened
at our spinning whetstone
lapidary disk in air

meant to make me glorious
his arms banded me
in our garden of scalding radishes

he fed the winter birds
and late at night he cooked for me
when I came home unkissed

how forgive the blows
he gave to others—
no logic to love's offices

Of Us

one never made it back
another circled far away
another was buried in a gray plot
one played an old-fashioned brass instrument
one made her hand into her heart
another made dolls with angry faces
one painted a black line

First Trip Since the Disaster

we see ourselves
in the black windows
rushing without moving

Cammy Thomas grew up on Long Island, New York. She graduated from the University of California, Berkeley, from which she also earned a PhD. She holds an MFA in creative writing from Warren Wilson College. She lives in Lexington, Massachusetts, with her husband and two daughters, and teaches English at Concord Academy.